Kevin is playing on the grass.

He sees a small red ball.

He picks it up and he runs off with it.

He sees Wellington sitting by a tall tree. Kevin drops the ball next to him. Wellington will not play. He tells Kevin to go away.

Kevin sees Lotty sitting by the wall.

He runs to play with her.

Lotty will not play.

She tells Kevin to go away.

Kevin is sad. No one will play with him. He kicks the small red ball. The small red ball hits the tree. Then it hits the wall.

Then it falls down the well.

Oh no! Kevin runs to the well.

He looks down it. Oh no!

Kevin falls down the well too.

"Help me, help me," yells Kevin. Wellington and Lotty run to the well.

"Look out," calls Wellington, as he pushes the bucket down the well.

Bump, bang, clang. Kevin gets into the bucket at the bottom of the well. Then Wellington and Lotty pull ... and pull ... and pull ...

They pull the bucket up to the top of the well. Kevin jumps out with the small red ball.

Oh no! The small red ball is flat.